"A Journey On The Path Called Life"

Soul Writings

By

The Universal Scribe

Order this book online at www.trafford.com/07-1822
or email orders@trafford.com

Most Trafford titles are also available at major online book retailers.

Note for Librarians: A cataloguing record for this book is available from Library and Archives Canada at www.collectionscanada.ca/amicus/index-e.html

ISBN: 978-1-4251-4351-0

We at Trafford believe that it is the responsibility of us all, as both individuals and corporations, to make choices that are environmentally and socially sound. You, in turn, are supporting this responsible conduct each time you purchase a Trafford book, or make use of our publishing services. To find out how you are helping, please visit www.trafford.com/responsiblepublishing.html

Our mission is to efficiently provide the world's finest, most comprehensive book publishing service, enabling every author to experience success. To find out how to publish your book, your way, and have it available worldwide, visit us online at www.trafford.com/10510

www.trafford.com

North America & international
toll-free: 1 888 232 4444 (USA & Canada)
phone: 250 383 6864 • fax: 250 383 6804
email: info@trafford.com

The United Kingdom & Europe
phone: +44 (0)1865 722 113 • local rate: 0845 230 9601
facsimile: +44 (0)1865 722 868 • email: info.uk@trafford.com

10 9 8 7 6 5 4 3

ACKNOWLEDGEMENTS

This book is written in appreciation of the many students and teachers who have crossed my path. To my parents, my family, my friends and coworkers, I kneel in gratitude at your feet for being in my life, for the love and lessons I have learned. You have helped make this lifelong dream, a reality!!

And to you, Florence, you have been my constant guide and inspiration.

Meegwetch to the Creator!

DEDICATION

To Sophie, Tessa and Sam – you are the lights in my life!

Through the winds of time
Love carries us.
The love of a mother for a daughter
The love of mother and child
And a grandmother's love
Echoes throughout eternity!

INTRODUCTION

POETRY—THE NECTAR OF THE GODS

My name is Marney Jamieson, the Universal Scribe.
And I've walked many paths
To be with you . . .
I've learned many lessons.
Been a student of great teachers
And I am here
As both a teacher and a student!

Many years ago in Ancient Egypt
Poetry was used to soothe the soul...
A nectar of the Gods.

Throughout the years
With my own writing, I have
Experienced the joy...
The sorrow...the passion
That poetry brings to me.

My poem (free verse)
"Because I am Me"
Was the first baby step of my writing
It taught me to stand tall in my integrity.

From there I've walked many avenues
Written when I'm inspired...
When I want to laugh...
When I feel my world has fallen apart...
Words flow and I find my answers.

My writing is a gift from my soul...
And through these readings
I trust that my writing will speak to your soul...
Awakening the passion within you
Helping you see your potential...
Assisting you to feel love...and overcome fear..
From my soul to yours...
Enjoy!!

July 2003

FORWARD

I hope you will join me on
This exciting Journey on a "Path called Life".
The journey is a source of learning...
The experience of walking the path...
The detours, the sabotage, the storms...
The lessons learned.
The relationships we create along the way
And the love we experience...
Learning to love ourselves
Truly love ourselves
Will bring a greater love to share with others.
Our Creator leads us on this wondrous journey
Through the joys, the sorrows, the trials and tribulations...
He's always there to hold our hand.
And...for me, the ultimate destination is
My eternal home.

Walk with me on the path
Feel the joy, the sorrow
The bliss
Of getting to know yourself.
The lessons leading you to greater enlightenment.

Everyone's journey is unique
As each one is unique
We all have a different walk
Other paths, separate detours...
But we are joined in love
As children of the Universe.

Delve to the depths of your soul
Learning to sing the song that is in your heart..

Shout your song from the mountain top.

Read and enjoy!
May peace be with you!

August 2007

Table of Contents

THE JOURNEY

There are many paths on life's journey...
You have a choice which path to take...

Ask the Creator for guidance in making the decisions.

Listen to your intuition!!!

The Path Called Life

Opportunities in my life
Have led me to be who I am.
Often I have walked alone
Feeling sad...
Feeling there was no one to guide me.

And then I felt that hand on my shoulder
A message to proceed
Telling me to go ahead...
That I'd be okay..
To take the leap...to stand alone!

I've learned that in order to be
Who I am...I must stand tall
Acknowledging my strengths...my courage
My willingness to be one amidst the crowd.
To be ME..
A person of integrity...a person of love..
A person who is loved.

Many may question the path I have chosen
The people who I call my friends...and
My deepest loves.
But I alone know what I have gained,
The hurts that I have felt,
But most important, the LOVE I have experienced...
The lessons I have learned.

For in the midst of my darkest shadows..
My deepest pain..
I give gratitude for what I have and,
What I have been given.

I, and I alone, must use the hand
That I have been dealt.
To make the choices that are best for me.
And while others may step blindly forward..
I will take that quiet moment of reflection
And then, with a smile on my face
Walk ahead...knowing I am not really alone.

A complex person, some may say
Others may question my choices.
But they are my choices...made from my beliefs.
Yes...I am a unique individual
Patterned by my experiences
Weathered by the storms...strengthened by my enduring faith.

I am a special person...
And, as each day enfolds
I am given greater wisdom to see who I really am!!!

If you wish to join me on this wondrous
Path called LIFE...you'll need courage and faith
A sense of adventure and a love of life
A willingness to share and care
And most of all..
A Belief that you do count
That you do make a difference!!

And through it all.. Know that Love is the greatest gift
That YOU deserve the best
That life has to offer.
(Believe it!!!)

December 1999.

THE JOURNEY

I started a walk today
That will last a lifetime.
The walk is about me
And what is best for me.

At times I may take baby steps...
Other times I'll be confident enough for giant steps..
But the focus will be on loving myself..
Doing the things that are best for me.

Loving myself not only means unconditional love..
But also loving myself with discipline.
Looking in the mirror and focusing on the love I feel
Makes me feel warm and glowing...
And oft times I forget the discipline..
The things I need to do for me.

It's easy to focus on the things I like...
And to feel that great love for me.
But discipline...that's a difficult one for me.

It means walking my talk.
If I truly love myself
I'll only fill my body with the nourishment
That is good for me...
That is healthy for my body.

Water will be a primary resource in my life
Just as in nature it plays an important role..
So in my body I require water to make my engine run.

Sleep is also important for me..
A good relaxed sleep...free of troubles.

I'll do a meditation or two before I sleep
And the focus will be on the positive.

Discipline will bring the balance in my life.
My mental health will thrive...
When I focus on the positive...
Work through my emotions and live in the "NOW"!
The past is gone..I'm learning my lessons..
And I'll no longer look in the rear view mirror!

Today is for living...I'll pray for guidance
Listen to my intuition and,
My connection with my higher power will guide me.
My spirituality is very important to me
And is only enhanced when I take
Loving care of myself.

As I walk through the woods
I enhance my physical well being..
Connect with nature...
Feel my energy rise..
And give thanks for the wonders I behold.

Taking care of my physical health is essential...
I notice the signs my body is giving me..
The need to rest more..the need to relax..
To release the tension.

And each step along the way I give thanks...
For my friends...the people I have met along my path..
My soul mates...
The lessons they have taught me...
And continue to teach me.

And I begin to realize my potential...
The love I have to give...
My creative power...
And what my creations will mean to myself and to others.

My walk helps me realize
The uniqueness that is me.
There is no one else like me!
I am a product of my background..
The walk...the path I have chosen.
The choices I make..
My teachers and the lessons I learn.

No one else will experience
Exactly what I do...
Feel the depths of my enthusiasm
The height of my passion for life.

And as I experience each step on this walk..
I raise my head in thanks..
Thanks for all I've been given..
For the great love of my life - ME
For my strength..my courage..my determination...
And most of all for the discipline I'm learning to use
To do what is best for me.

Walk the walk..
To greater heights.
Live your life to the fullest..
Be all that you can be.

The walk is your walk..
Your journey for the rest of your life.
What an experience!

January 2000

The Hill

I stood on the hill
Overlooking the frozen lake...
And the vision of such beauty
Took my breath away...

My mind wondered and I saw the scene in spring...
The water a vivid blue...encased in ice..
The grass so green...the beginning of a new season...
And I felt hope.

Deep within my heart feels frozen...
So encased in sorrow...
That it feels like the thaw will never come...
I'd like to retreat and leave the pain behind...
The pain of living...the memories...
The yesterdays...that cannot be today.

The smile I'll never see again...
The jokes never to share...
The love...oh...the love...
Never to feel again.

And yet...as I visualized the scene in spring...
I know that my heart will thaw...
That the pain will come and go...
That I will breath new life into my soul...

For life is not a game...
It's a path to follow...a river to cross...a hill to climb..
It's laughter and tears...
Joy and sorrow...
Beginnings and endings...

And it's love...eternal love...
That sustains us through the toughest times...

Our life on the earth is but a moment..
A brief moment in the realm of time...
A time for each of us to make a difference...

To sing the song that is in our hearts...
To delve to the depths of our soul...
To listen to our heart song..
And soar to our highest peaks...

We may be on this earth for a few years...
Or for a century...
But the quality of our life is what is important...
To live each moment..
To cherish each breath that we breathe...

To shout from the hilltops...
To live our lives with passion...
To enjoy each moment...

I feel my heart thawing...
As I look across the frozen lake...
Soon it will be Spring...

And as I walk away from the hill...
I look down...
And see the endless beauty...

Whatever season of the year...
Wherever I am in my life...
Love is the answer...

Love melts the ice within ...
And offers me the promise of a new day...

Yes, today there is sadness...

And yet...there is gratitude...
For that inner wisdom...
That helps me through each day...
That lets me feel...
And gives me hope for
Tomorrow.

I will journey to my favourite hill
On many a day...
To view the changing seasons...
To enjoy my life...
To just be...
Living for the moment...
And simply being me!!!.

March 2003

A WALK OF GRATITUDE

I started a walk today..
A walk of gratitude..
A walk of humility.

Giving thanks for who I am
For you have shown me
My beauty, my grace
My intelligence
The unique person that I am.

I am on this path
You have chosen for me
In order to write
I must feel the pain..
The joy
And realize who I am.

I see this beautiful creature
Walking towards me
Her head held high
And I am in awe.

She looks so confident
Walking tall
And she has a purpose
It's easy to see.

There is wisdom in her
And glory in her heart.

And as she moves
I realize it's me!

And I truly see the wonder
That is me.

Thank you – Meegwetch
For allowing me a glimpse
Of the person I am.
The person I am striving to become.

As she passes by..
I sigh. . .and I know
That she is me
And I am humbled!

June 2007

AND THE RIVER FLOWS

And the river flows
The river of my tears
And I know not why.

I feel that I don't have a place
That I don't belong
That I am alone
And I wonder about these feelings.

And the river flows
The river of my tears!

And the river forms
part of my writing..
The yearning to be
The yearning to know…
The longing…

And the emptiness
The emptiness
That stretches to eternity…

The eternity of my soul…
For I have neglected me…
The core of my being…
My needs…
My desires.

And have attempted to fill these needs
With the needs,
The desires of others…
And I know that their journey is not mine…
That they are on a different path…

And the only person to make me truly happy
Is me…
My writing…
And the journey to the depths of my being
To listen
To feel…
And connect!

And the answers will come…
The emptiness will be filled.

The love that emanates from the core or my being
Will bring me inner peace…
What I am longing for.

For many a year I have known…
That when I am caught up in the outside world
With it's superficial demands..
I feel a sense of aloneness…
A feeling of not belonging…
And I am sad…

The answer for me…
And will continue to be…
Is in my writing…
Delving to the depths…

Then, and only then…
Can I truly…can I truly belong…
Can I truly be…
True to me.

Yes, I long to be one of the pack…
But this is not for me…
For I must be the person I am meant to be…
And I…and only I…
Know this person!

And the river flows..
The river of my tears…
And I feel a sense of happiness
That has been missing…

For the answer is within…
Found in the journey to my soul!!!

And the river flows
The river of my tears…
The warmth flowing and
Washing away my fears!!!

June 2007

MY GOLDEN YEARS

I look in the mirror
And see a face...
Familiar...and yet can this be me??
At times I feel so young...
The face in the mirror...who is she?

My face reflects the journeys of my life.
The lines around my eyes...
Tell of the times I have laughed...
As well as when I've cried.
The wrinkles...they tell of my experiences...
The path I've walked.

I am still so beautiful...
But the inner me....my youthful self...
Is the true me.

I walk with dignity...strong in who I am...
Being young was wonderful...
But now I have the wisdom and courage
To enjoy each day...
The beauty of the sunrise...
The magnificent sunset..

Walking in the rain is a wondrous experience...
My bones may ache...but to walk..
To enjoy nature...is part of the rapture of life.

Yes...I've come a long way...
Walked many paths...
Met many people...
Have known a lifetime of love...

Each day is a new experience...
A treasure to enjoy...

They are truly the golden years of my life.

May 2003

A PRECIOUS GIFT

I walk through life..
Expecting the path to be smooth...
That everything will go the way I wish..
And when it doesn't..
I have often been distraught...
Crying out...**WHY ME?**
What did I do to deserve this!!

As I learn to view the ripples
or the bumps on my path
As lessons to be learned...
Perhaps to make me stronger...
More compassionate...
Making me dip into my inner resources..
I am amazed at the outcome.

I am not the same person...
Outwardly I may look the same...
But there is more depth...
Because I have reached into my very soul
For the answers.

The path takes on new meaning...
Sure, I'd like smooth sailing...
But the bumps...the waves...
Offer me challenges...
Sometimes even adventure...
And provide me with a different way of viewing the world.

This week has had unique meaning for me...
I have questioned who I am...
where I've been...and where I'm going....
And the answers I have received..

Make me think of Easter...

It's never too late....
The dawning of a new day
Offers each of us an opportunity to begin anew
To be reborn...
To live life to the fullest...
With gratitude in our hearts....
To see every step on our path...as a precious gift!!!!

April 2001

WOMEN OF THE EARTH

It is our time
To make a difference…
Listen to Mother Earth
Feel her pulse
The pulse of the universe.

Listen to the wind sing
To the birds chirp
To the water of life
Listen to their cries…
of desperation
Keep us safe
Preserve us.

And my body quivered
And I was in ancient times
A cave woman…
Feeling the pulse of the world
As my heart pulsed,
The world pulsed
I was the centre of the universe.

The rivers called and I answered
They told me stories
Of my creation
And told of the future…

Of the wonder of fire
For warmth
And to beware
Fire warms the soul
But can also destroy the world.

And listen to the peace
Listen to your heart
Hug a tree…feel the love.
And know you are never ..never alone.

And a rainbow appeared
And the world was my horizon
As I ventured forth
A wonderland to behold.

And Mother Earth in all her glory
Beckoned me
To discover…to explore..
To be in her wonderland.

My cave is no longer my home
As I venture on…
Feel the earth's warmth
The streams…a gift from the gods..
Feeding my body
And nourishing my soul.

And the animals become my family and teachers
The wolf teaches me of family
And the eagle flies…soaring free.
As free as I feel.

And I lie on Mother Earth
And I am cocooned by her.

And she whispers to me
"I will always be with you
Take care of me
As I take care of you
Nourish me
As I nourish you.

Feel my heartbeat

Blending with yours
And know that you are never alone."

The cave has been left behind
I'm beginning a new Journey
But Mother Earth will be with me always
As I venture on this wondrous journey of discovery

And the wind whistles
And the wolf howls..

As I soar free!

January 2003

LESSONS

Your Journey through life is unique...
It's yours to celebrate.

Learn the lessons you've been given.

When the student is ready...
The teacher appears!!!!

IN THE NOW

I live in the now.
Yesterday…is just that… Yesterday
Tomorrow may never come.

I am focused on this moment
Truly being me
In the place I am meant to be
Living the moment to the fullest
And feeling a sense of peace.

Yesterday I would have been worrying
About all the yesterdays
About today and
What will happen tomorrow?

Today I realize
Living in the now
Gives me a sense of security
Of calm
I have never experienced.

I feel my beauty
My magnificence
And my uniqueness…

In the now..
One with the universe

NOW!!!!

July 2007

PUPPET ON A STRING

For many a year I've let others pull my strings
I've been content to be what they wanted
They pulled the strings controlling my head and my heart
And I nodded "yes".

Yes, I agree.
Yes that's what I want..
I am in total agreement with all of the above.
Which restaurant would you like to eat in...
It doesn't matter...
Anything is OK with me.

My strings have been pulled in so many ways.
My mind manipulated...my heart broken.
Left to fall in tiny pieces...
Pieces that only I can pick up and put together again.

I thought that if I was agreeable...
Everything would work out...
If I played the game..
That I would be accepted.
But it didn't matter any way!!!

So today...in anger, fighting for my own integrity
My values...my dignity..
I grabbed the strings and tried to run...
Run from everything I had ever known...
Had ever cared about.
Feeling so fragile...certainly like a puppet...
Left to pull my own strings.

My run was like a drunken brawl..
I needed to learn to walk all over agin.

No one has been there for me for a long time...
So who has been controlling my strings...
I have..of course.

But when I get in difficult situations
Or when I feel uncertain
I give the strings to someone else to pull.
Then what I do is for them..Not for me.
Wanting them to like me...
To care for me...
To think I'm OK...
To accept me.

Today, as I stagger along...falling to my knees.
I say a prayer asking for guidance...
Giving me the strength and courage to stand tall..
To start pulling my own strings..
To let my heart open...feel the pain...
Go with it...cry, and as I empty
I will be replenished with positive energy.

Learning to pull my own strings will be
A great learning exercise for me.
It will be an hourly venture
Remembering to do what is best for me.
I have a great mind, wisdom and determination..
I need to keep this in the forefront.

When I fall backwards and once again become a puppet
I'll pick myself up and start again.

Being a puppet is not fun!!
We can't continually dance to someone else's tune.
We have to dance to our own...
To do as our heart guides us.

Puppets are controlled by others!!
I will no longer accept this...

At times I may be very lonely...
People who have been on my path
May no longer accept me for who I am.
But I am my own person.

And as I learn to love myself
To take care of myself...
To look in the mirror and affirm this love.
I will learn to do what is best for me.

Loving myself is the only answer
I can no longer be on a pendulum
Dictated by the wishes of others.
I need to pull my own strings..
To no longer be a victim...
To talk tall...
Standing in my own integrity.

It may be fun to play with puppets
But only if they're toys.
People...myself included..
Need to be treated with respect and integrity...
To be valued for who we are.

Remember, when you feel someone pull your strings
–You are not a puppet
–You do have a choice
–A choice to be who you want to be
–A choice to do what you want to do.
–To be the best person you can be!!

Your influence in the world will be much stronger!!
As an autonomous individual
You have much to give the world
Spreading your love to those around you.

Once in a while you'll feel a tug
But that's OK ...look in the mirror and smile

And sing...

"Once upon a time..
I was a puppet on a string
Now I'm a beautiful bird and I can fly
And I love me!!!"

June 2000

ASK...AND I WILL RECEIVE

Inside my body
I feel a mound...
So solid
So hard...
I can barely breathe...

And when I shout...
What a release!
The mound gets smaller...
But only for a little while
And then it grows larger.

And over the years...
It has grown to fill me...
It is encompassing my heart...
My soul.

And today I realized
That this mound...
This mass within me...
That has been consuming me...
Is anger...
So intense
So devastating...
That it is destroying me.

So for now...
I will make the choice to release this anger...
If only for a moment.

I visualize the anger as a large ball
I remove it and place it in a box...

And look at it from a distance…
I wonder what it means…
But I'll leave it there for a while.

And suddenly, I feel so light…
So empty…
And yet, it's a good emptiness…
I feel like I've lost a burden…
A heavy weight has lifted…

And sometime,
When I'm in the right place
and the proper space
I'll look at this object in the box…
But only when I'm ready…

And when I feel this heavy weight inside…
I'll take the time…
To visually put it in a box…

Anger…resentment…bitterness
Are emotions…
I need to deal with…

And eventually I'll let go and
Let God…

Forgiveness is a part…
Ask and I shall receive…

November 2006

NO

All my life
I've tried to be the good person..
The person everyone likes
The one who is oh..so agreeable
Going along with what others want!

No back bone you say...
No that's not how I see myself...
I'm certainly no coward..
But I truly don't like arguments
I like to be liked by everyone...of that there is no doubt.
Never the centre of a crowd....
A person on the outside...
Just content to be me.

And today I had to take a closer look at me
Why things happen to me...
Why I feel this vast void.

Going along with the world....
Keeping a silent voice....
Certainly isn't making me happy.

No matter what I do or where I go
These doubts ..this uncertainly goes with me.

All the times I say YES - I agree...
My pleasant smile..my loving ways
Aren't working for me.

And I had to take a moment to search my soul
To find out why...
And the answer instantly appeared....

I have to learn to say NO.

No to the things that are not good for me.
No to what feels wrong for me.
Regardless of other people's reactions
Regardless of their opinion of me..
Courting their favour...isn't making my world secure.

The answer is all about me
Thinking enough of myself...
Having the courage...
And most of all...
Loving myself enough
To say **NO!!**

I may have to take small steps at first...
And then as I progress...larger ones...
And eventually I'll run....
And maybe even fly!!!!

Why...because today I realize
It's not about anyone else
It's about me!

Whether I like myself enough...
Whether I love myself enough...
To dare to be me...

To respect my decisions...my opinions
And say NO to what feels wrong for me...
And a loud YES to what is good for me!!!!!!!!!

Another lesson...
On the path called LIFE.

July 2000

LETTING GO

What does this mean to me?
It means letting go of
All my hopes and dreams..
Of a life with someone I love..
Knowing that I can never be with him again
Letting go of the hope that it could be otherwise.

It means loneliness...even emptiness
Yes, loneliness has become part of my life..
But this means releasing a part of my life
Occupied by those hopes and dreams.

It leaves me vulnerable..
Very open..
Feeling sad...unsure...
Abandoned..

And yet...open!!
Open to new challenges
Possibly in time to a new love...
The opportunity for new dreams
New goals..

Closing the door allows me
To open a new one...
There is fear...
And risk in taking that giant step...
It is easier to cling to the old...
Regardless of the pain..
At least there is something...not emptiness...

Clinging to the pain is easier

Than saying NO
And walking away!!!

Letting go ultimately is all about me!
It is the end of punishing myself
For a situation that didn't work out...
Yes...it was my dream...
But it has to be someone else's as well..

This lesson...as I put pen to paper..
I realize is one of my greatest ones...
I have to let go...I don't want to!!!
But I deserve new hopes and dreams...
And my passion for this new way of life
Is stronger
Than my desire to cling to the past.

May 2001

THE SENSUAL ME!!

I've often wondered why
I don't feel loved...
Why I don't feel fulfilled.
I want a relationship..
And yet, when I'm in one
The loneliness is still there...
My needs are not met.

And I realized it's about
Loving all aspects of me.
I've learned to love my tenderness...
My kindness...the essence of my soul..
My abilities...my spirituality...

But my physical needs
Or shall I be so bold
As to say, sexual..
That has been taboo.

I have pretended they're not part of me
I've held myself apart
From this passionate side of my nature.
I look at couples...and I want to be
Part of a couple, too.
And then everything will be okay.

And then I remember the other relationships..
And what went wrong and I realize
I have to really love myself
Not just my inner being
But the outer self...my body.

I have to become familiar with myself
From the top of my head
To the tips of my toes...
To know my erroneous zones...
To pleasure myself...
Love myself...as a lover would..

Be gentle...be kind...
Say those special words of endearment...
And give those secretive looks in the mirror...
Those touches in a seductive manner...
Teasing...tantalizing...arousing me.
The essence of who I am...
A person capable of immense passion
And an abundance of love.

And the tears fall
And my heart bursts
Because just thinking of this love
Humbles me..possibly brings me
To another time and place...
But I can do this for me..
Really love me.
I'm an expert at loving my inner beauty...
Now I'll learn to appreciate my external beauty.

I can have it all
If only I have the courage
To know what I want...
To believe I deserve it..
And it will be mine!!

And I'll know the type of love
I have only envisioned
The love will be unconditional
I'll pamper myself knowing, as only I can,
What pleases me.

The wonder...the excitement of
Being loved by someone who knows my every need...
Inside and out...
Someone who has known me all my life...
Has walked the same path
Shed the same tears...
And has learned to love all parts of me.

There is adventure every day...
In every way.
Whether walking alone or with someone else
The sun shines brighter...
The world is more vibrant..
When I love myself...
Truly love me for who I am!!!!!!!

April 2001

TRUSTING MYSELF

So many times in my life
I've made decisions
Based on what I thought would be better for others.
I've run from situations..
Haven't fought for things..
Because I felt others had more to offer.

When will I grow up and realize
That if someone really loves me
They will appreciate me for me.
I don't have to offer anything but me...
It's called unconditional love.

And then I said to myself
Perhaps I have to look in my heart
and find out whether I like me...
Love me...feel I'm worthwhile.

When I learn to truly love me
My situation will change
I'll be more confident
Realizing that I alone hold the key..

So today's lesson..
As so many lessons in my life
Has rocked me to the core

I fought it...
I ran...I climbed the highest peaks to escape the answer...
Failing to look for the solution
Until it knocked me to my knees.

The solution is me

I hold it inside me!!!

I often struggle...
Fighting my feelings..
Not realizing what is wrong..

When I know that deep inside of me
I hold the key!

And for me..
When I feel agitated...
When I feel lonely..
When I feel overwhelmed
And I know not why..

I have only to put a pen in my hand
And the answer appears...
So profoundly...so instantaneous
It's a miracle.

And yet...so many times I hesitate...
Running from pillar to post
Searching for an answer
Looking for a response.

And yet, afraid to lift that pen
Afraid to see what I will uncover.

I guess we're all like that
We pick up a book..
We seek advice from others...
Not a bad habit I'll admit
But we all reach a point in our lives
When we need to sit in silence
To look within...
And the answers will appear.

And often when we search the world over...

Rather than looking within
It's because we don't trust ourselves...
Trust our wisdom...
Trust our knowledge.

Trusting myself is so important
It's an important lesson on the path of loving myself
In respecting my knowledge..
My intuitive power
Believing in myself
And feeling that I am worthwhile!

July 2000

QUEST

Often I wish
That I could accept things as they are.
That I didn't search for deeper meaning in life.
It would be so simple not to question
Not to look beneath the surface...
To just settle.

When I feel this gnawing inside...
This quest from my soul..
Whispering to me
"Be all that you can be"...
I build a wall and close my ears
And try to be content with the way I am..
And the way things are!!

Lately, I haven't been able to keep the wall up...
It's crumbling fast and furious
And I'm glad!

I can no longer be that good little girl
Trying so hard to please others...
For now I have to please me!

And strangely enough it's not so difficult
When I really listen to me.
What I want and need
Can't be measured on any scale
Or be satisfied by monetary gain.

My needs are universal
Love...fulfilment
A sense of self
Of gratitude
Of humility!!!!!

October 2000

GRATITUDE

On this Thanksgiving weekend
I have so much to be thankful for
Where do I start?

I give thanks for the air that I breathe...
The food that I eat...
My home..
Good friends...
The people I work with...
My family...and the new member
Who I'll meet next week.

My little companion Princess, my dog...

But most of all I give thanks for the beauty that surrounds me...
The wonder of it all...
The life I have been given..
The opportunity to make choices...
The lessons I have to learn...
The pleasure...the pain...
The ability to feel...
The bliss...the sorrow.
The miraculous connection with the Creator.

Thanksgiving is celebrated this weekend
But every day of the year...
I give thanks and gratitude for what I've been given..
The bounties that have been bestowed on me..

My riches lie not in my possessions..
But in my experiences..
The love that surrounds me ...
The depth of my connection with the divine...

On this Thanksgiving weekend...
I say a special thank you...
Gratitude has shaped my life..
And enhanced my journey.

I am humbled by the riches
I continue to receive!!!

October 2002

MY PRESCRIPTION

I have been struggling so long...
Today I cried...
Why aren't things different...
I long for someone in my life?

I talked to a friend and
Told her of my woes.
How my life never seems to get better...
I go to the Circle every week...
And feel so wonderful...
There is so much love.

At the Circle, I write..I sing...I dance...
And leave there feeling so content.
And for a day or two I feel serene...
And then the walls cave in...
I am down again...
Yearning for things to be different.

Today I sat and meditated
And felt so peaceful..
This is how I feel in the Circle...
And I suddenly realized
For me it has to be an every day occurrence...
I need to find my prescription to keep me going...
To make my life complete.

I have learned so much
And I have to apply it daily
Working on all aspects of my being...
Loving myself...Caring for me...

The world may not change

But I will
I'll attract different people
My world will be brighter
Because I am taking care of me.

My prescription for my life
Is mine alone...
Music reaches my soul...
Making me come alive...
Giving enriches me...
Meditation takes me to another world...
Prayer is my foundation.

Working on myself daily
Makes it easier to face life's realities
My tensions are lessened
My world broader.

My prescription will become
My foundation for living
It costs only moments of my time
Yet the benefits are miraculous..
I have to renew the prescription regularly
Changing it when needed.

I will develop my prescription for life...
Because I am worth it..
I want things to change...
And I have the tools to make it happen.

I need to use the tools I've been given
And these tools will set me free!!

November 2002

LOVE

Love brings joy...
A never ending sense of peace...
As we soar through eternity!!!!!

MY CHILD

I felt you move within my womb
And our love was forever bound.
As I nourished you...
I felt complete and you became a part of me.
For nine months I carried you
And when you were born.
I saw an angel!!

Such beauty...so vital and aware.
You were a child of the Creator..
And you were mine, if only for a little while.

I held you at my breast
And I felt a tingling
a feeling of wonder...
And as you suckled..
Our bond grew stronger.

I watched you grow...
Heard your cries of anger...of hunger...
Saw your first smile..
And with each new development...
For me it was a miracle..
And you are my miracle..my child.

You rolled over
And soon you crawled...
And then you were standing...
And the next moment you were walking...

Each was a new adventure
I saw life through your eyes...
The innocence...the wonder...the rapture.

You laughed at a worm
Crawling on the sidewalk.
Jumping in puddles was your delight.
When you sat at the table.
Your eyes begging for one more cookie..
How could I refuse!!

Each new development...
Each step along the way...
We walked together..
And suddenly you wanted independence
To ride your own bike...
To walk across the street to see a friend..
And I was not a part.

You'd come running home..
To tell me all about it...
What you'd been doing...
Your eyes bright with fire..
And your world was expanding..

You listened to me...sometimes
But you had your own ideas...
oh yes...and there were many.

School was your great adventure
New friends...new activities
And suddenly you were on your own.

Gone all day...
Not needing me as much...
Those days flew by...
One day you were five...
And I turned around and you were twelve...
A young woman...an adolescent.

You're still in my life
You'll always be.

I close my eyes and
Feel you suckling on my breast
I see your first smile
And I know I'll have you only for a little while.

Children are God's angels
Given to us on loan
They enrich our lives
And teach us unconditional love.

April 2002

HIS HAND

I was sinking...drowning in an ocean of loneliness
I felt a hand...
Reaching for mine...
The touch reached my very soul...
Warming my heart and making me feel secure.

I felt like a child
Holding her father's hand.
While I clutched tight
I was secure
Loved, and oh...so soft and warm...
I was safe!

And as I raised my head
I looked into a pair of the most loving eyes.
It was my Father...my Creator...
And I was a child once again
So loved...so cherished.

The love was unconditional
And the feeling of love shining from His eyes...
Resonated to my very soul...
Ending my loneliness and longing.

We walked together for a while..
Hand in hand...
Talking...laughing and simply being...
It felt like we'd been together
Throughout eternity.

I felt Him release my hand
And I awoke from my dream..
Feeling warm and cuddly..

Like a child awakening from a nap.

And a tiny voice within whispered...
He is always with me..
Offering comfort, love and support...
As I walk on my journey...
Through this path called "life"

July 2003

FALLING IN LOVE

A friend once said..
Loving yourself will be
The greatest gift you will ever receive.

Oh, yes, I replied
With doubt in my voice
That will be the day!

And for many years she's been patient with me...
Knowing that when the time was right...
I'd follow her advice.
She's one of the greatest teachers of my life.

Look into the mirror she said
And behold the woman that is you.
Look at yourself and...
Tell yourself how much **You love YOU.**
Set your timer for 10 minutes and begin.

I'll certainly do that...I replied with a smile on my face
As she went out the door...
I approached the mirror with great trepidation.

I stood there looking into my eyes...
I wanted to run...
I wanted to hide...
But I bravely looked ahead staring into
A pair of beautiful eyes.

And the tears started to fall on to my cheeks
I said....
You're so beautiful
You're so lovable
I'll never desert you
I'll always be there

Regardless of the wrinkles on your face or
The colour of your hair!

I'll always love you
You're the love of my life.
I'll stay with you forever.
When your teeth begin to rattle and
Your memory fades I'll still be there!

And as I continued to stare at the person in the mirror
I could tell she felt the same love as I did.
I hugged myself as the tears fell on my cheeks.

I'll never be alone..
There'll always be someone who loves me...
And, that's ME!!!!

And, since that day
When my dear friend said...ten minutes or more..
I've been looking in the mirror
And admiring the beauty of my greatest love...ME.

Sometimes I smile and sometimes I cry
For the feelings are so intense.
I have never known a love as great as this.

And yesterday, when I was sitting in my chair
I heard a voice say..
I love you...you're the greatest!
I looked behind me..
And there was no one there..
For the voice was from inside!

Imagine... this precious gift could be yours.
Take the risk...look in the mirror
At the wonder that is YOU.
Fall in love with yourself!!!!

January 2000

GOD'S SPIRIT

And God's Spirit is in
Each of us…
Calling us…
Whispering our name
You are loved…
Truly loved.

You are my child..
Walk with me..
Talk with me..
Hold my hand
And venture forth..
You are not alone.

Take that step
That will lead you to
Your highest potential.

My child…you are a gift
A wondrous creature.
You are a miracle!
Always walk your truth
And you will go far.

Your gift is a wonder for all
To know.

Sing from the hill tops
Run in the rain
Remain my child forever.

There will never be another
Just like you.

Dance…take that step..

Sing the song that
Is in your heart.

You are a part of me
My precious child
You are never alone.

Rejoice in knowing
You are loved
Adored and
Will one day be home.

My precious child..
My angel!

And the angels sang
And the harps played
A tune. . .just for me.

You have journeyed long and far
For others
Now the journey is for you.

To learn who you are
To learn of your beauty
Your potential
The love you have to give
The precious gift that you are.

And we sing to you our special song
Created by our heavenly choir.

"Rejoice my child
Rejoice my child
Rejoice in who you are
You've walked so many miles
Shed so many tears
But now you're free!

Rejoice my child
Rejoice my child
Rejoice in who you are.

You are adored
You are loved
Enjoy the freedom
Walk in your glory
Walk in your light.

Rejoice my child
Rejoice my child
Rejoice in who you are.

And a light shines for you
A vibrant light
Will show you the way.

Rejoice my child
Rejoice

And one day my child
You will be home again
Part of our heavenly choir.

So rejoice in who you are
A precious gift

Rejoice my child
Rejoice
Your beauty
Your serenity
Will last throughout time.

Rejoice in God's grace
Rejoice
Rejoice!"

March 2007

THE ENCOUNTER

I walked through the door at the office
And saw them in a brief embrace…
My heart fluttered…
My stomach ached
And my soul sang!

I felt the love between the two
And it affected me to my very core.

I joked about the encounter…
And yet it was no joke..
It was so beautiful that
It brought tears to my eyes.

It was the essence of love…
Sharing…letting love flow…
Daring to take a risk…
Being spontaneous!

And for me…I realize
That love has many forms
And can be shown in many ways…
By an embrace
By a touch
By a look
By a smile
By listening to music
By acts of kindness..
The ways are endless.

And as I venture further on life's path
I appreciate the miracle of love..
Life's greatest gift.

I welcome it. . .cherish it..
Love warms my soul
And fills every cell of my body!

There are many types of love
For a friend
For a parent. . .
For a partner
For a child
Love of life. . .
And love of self.
And I truly believe that the cycle of love is enhanced
By loving yourself!
The encounter was so profound. . .
Part of the wonderful cycle of love!

January 2004

LOVE IS A CHOICE

I once wrote a poem
'Puppet on a String'
And that's what I have allowed myself to be...

I go along for a while and I am in control..
And then something happens...and I am
being pulled by another...
Someone is pulling my strings...
The feeling is devastating...
It is as if I have no control of myself...
My behaviour...
My life...
I am living totally for someone else.

It may be past life karma...but it has to end...
I need myself back...to make my decisions
Based on what is best for me..
I will pull my own strings...
And not be led by the wishes of others.

It has nothing to do with caring for others...
It has everything to do
With caring for myself...

I have danced to another's tune for too long...
My life has evolved around
what is happening in another's life...
It's time I stood tall...
Acknowledged my feelings...
And took control of my destiny...

The anger...the uncertainty, the soul wrenching pain
Of these past weeks..

Is my choice...
And I no longer want to live this way...

I have so much to offer the world...
But my vision has been clouded...
My energy sapped by giving to another...
I refuse to be a puppet on a string...
I deserve to be first in my life...
To love and honour myself...
What is happening around me is insignificant..
Compared to what is happening within...
Feeling my beauty...
The love I have for myself...
Listening to the voice from my inner core...
And going for it.

The voice from my inner core...
No longer whispers to me...
It has been shouting...
What about me?
Where do I fit?
I am repeating old patterns...
And pulling myself apart.

I care ...I love...
But what about me?
My beauty and potential have been blocked
By another...

No...I am not a puppet...
I am allowing myself to be controlled...
And this will stop...

Why...because I care about me...
I love myself...
And I am a cherished child of the Creator.

And the song that is in my heart...

Is waiting to be sung...
From the highest treetops...

Love is eternal...
Love is everlasting...
Love is unconditional...
Love is a choice...

And my choice is to love me first...
And the rest of the world will follow!

December 2002

POWER OF POWER

I stood in a large auditorium
Having just finished the teaching of a lifetime
And I felt power of power...
I was embraced by love.

Can you imagine?
Being in a circular auditorium
The love flowing from me to everyone in attendance...
Their love flowing back to me...

And the love flowing to the walls
And vibrating...resonating...
And filling every corner of the auditorium
And every core of our being.

The power of power
Is love building on love
Love, the strongest force on earth
Can break down walls...
Can erase prejudice...
Can heal the deepest wounds...
Can set us free!

Imagine, if this love filled the world
Resonating from every corner of the universe
Each of us would be wrapped in a cocoon of love.

This is what the Creator wishes for all of us.
Unconditional love...
Love surrounding us
Never ending love
And this is our greatest gift.

October 2003

IT'S BETWEEN GOD AND I!!

When it seems like the world
Has been ripped from beneath my feet
And I have no where to turn…
My answer lies with God.

Everything changes…
Relationships will end.
But my relationship with the Creator is everlasting.
My Creator is my strength and inspiration.

Today, the rug was ripped
From beneath my feet…
My stable life is gone.
What now?

God has a plan for me…
And I have to believe and trust
That everything will work out…
That the resources will be provided…
That the master plan
Will bring me wonders
Difficult for me to comprehend at this time!

God's love will surround
And protect me.
I am not alone.
I will not fight this battle alone.
I will be given the strength
To walk forward with my head held high
And a new chapter in my life will unfold.

My Creator…
My Strength and Inspiration…
My Dearest Friend!!!

December 2005

ON THE WINGS OF HAPPINESS

From the moment I met you I saw the beauty within
The wonderful person that you are...
The bird struggling to be free.

I know that there have been struggles...
Your life has been a series of lessons to be learned
And you have grown into a dynamic individual
Standing tall in your integrity.

When you told me about your upcoming marriage
I saw a light in your eyes...brighter than any star.
You were a young child...so happy...so in love..
And your face radiated with your happiness.

And I reflected on life's greatest gift "Love"
And how important it is in all our lives.

You have been friends and lovers
For so many years...
and the bond has been strengthened
by your friendship and love.

And your marriage...the binding of your relationship
Before the Creator and your friends...
Is for the two of you alone.

For you have worked together to make this a union
Cherished by yourselves.
And a creation of rare beauty in the eyes of the Creator.

You are two birds flying free

On the wings of your happiness!!!
Congratulations!
Know how much I care!

March 2004

DETOURS

Remove the fear from your life…

Replace it with love…

Dare to live!!!

Imagine the freedom of being anything
You want to be!!!!!

STORMS

And the wind blew...
The thunder rolled
And the lightning shot through the sky...
And I stood in trepidation
Wondering what was coming next!

Storms...are a part of our external life...
And our internal life as well.
External storms can be frightening and
Yet so beautiful...

The rain pattering on the roof...
On a warm summer's day...
The rainbow that follows...
Brings new hope and joy.

A winter storm
Leaves the world encased
In a wonderland of snow...
A miracle has changed the landscape.

And as I journey inward
I remember the storms of my life...
When I took a walk on a new path...
The fear...the challenge...
And the joy when I made new friends...
Accomplished my dreams...
And felt the passion of living
In every cell of my being.

This passion in me...
Is like thunder and lightning...
I am calm for a while...

And then it breaks loose...
And I have learned...
That I have to go with it...
Someone else is in control.

My passion takes many forms...
But the most enjoyable one
Is my writing...
I take a pen in hand...
Start to write...
Never knowing what is to come...
And the emotions flow onto the paper...
And my heart does flip flops...

Wondering where this is coming from???
And the end result is the miracle...
My rainbow...
My writing...
A gift from my soul.

There have been many storms in my life...
And learning to go with it...
Not to fight is the answer...
With my feet planted firmly on the ground...
I walk onward...
With my hand in the Creator's...

The path may not be the one
I thought I was to take...
But the wonders of the experiences...
Are the lessons I am meant to learn.

How can I forget
The joy and pain of
My first love...
The birth of my child...

The wonder of a love affair and

The end of my dream
Of a lifelong marriage...

The courage and determination
I have used time and time again...
To venture forth
Into uncharted territory.

The storms in my life...
External and internal...
Are the miracles in my life..
I have learned many valuable lessons...
Walked many miles...
Many of them alone.

I see myself...
With eyes that penetrate to my very soul...
Asking why...
And yet...knowing...
That after every storm a rainbow will appear...
A rainbow just for me...
It will surround me with love...
And healing...
While I lie in the Creator's arms.

November 2002

CHANGES

My life is ever changing...
Just when I think I have all the questions answered..
New ones appear...
New challenges are on the horizon.

I need to build a foundation
for my life...
A foundation that will maintain me...
Through the good times and the bad...
A foundation built of faith, strong principles, beliefs
a love of my Creator...
and unconditional love of myself.

I am not the job I currently hold
The clothes I wear...
The car I drive...
The home I live in...
I am that child who resides within...
Ever knowing...ever loving.

Keeping this child warm and loved
Will keep me secure...
Through all the trials and tribulations of my life.

There will be losses...
There will be pain...
The foundation of my beliefs
Will carry me through!!

Tomorrow will be a sunny day
Because I feel a strong sense of purpose
Of why I am here.

No one can take that from me.
I am loved and I am loving...
And I am here to carry this love to others..

Every day is a new day...
A chance to begin again
Yes, there will be changes...
But my daily prescription
Will help me through the day.

My prescription..
Time spent in meditation
A diet of healthy food...
Water...the essence of life...
A good night's sleep
Love...companionship...friendship..
Exercise..
And time spent with my Creator.

Yes my life is changing...
Yesterday is gone forever
And as I step forward
The foundation I have built will carry me
Through happiness and sorrow.

And the changes...
Allow me the opportunity to grow..
To see new horizons.
Challenges allow me to develop my potential
To sing the song that is in my heart
Carrying me on my journey.
I see a rainbow above me...
A new world beckoning...
Calling me to venture forth...
To explore...

And I take the step into the unknown...

Knowing that I am Okay...
That I'll survive...

The fear evaporates
and I fly!!

July 2003

SABOTAGE

My life has taken many twists and turns..
I walk a straight line for a while..
And suddenly I am hurling down a path
I've never known before!

Why, when things seem to be going so well
Does everything go in a tail spin?
When my future looks so bright…
Do I walk into a dark tunnel?

I know that there will be ups and downs in my life…
But I still ask why and I go to my inner core
For the answer.

Yes, there are life's lessons to learn…
But my inner gut feeling tells me
This is not about that…
It's about me loving myself.

For a while I do everything I need to do for me…
I am the priority…
And then I start to slip…
Doing only a few things a day..
And eventually nothing for myself..
And then...
My world takes a dive.

I focus on the world around me...
Not on my inner core..
I start doing things that harm me..
Making decisions that are not good for me…
Why…when I have the daily prescription I need
Do I sabotage???

The answer is…
I need to love myself unconditionally.
Until I make this declaration to myself…
Think it…feel it in my soul
And in every cell of my body…
I will sabotage my well being.

Have I ever believed that I am worth
A life full of joy and love?
Yes, when I meditate and am completely still…
I feel this love…
And then the world creeps in…
And my decisions are not always good for me.

My inner core…
My true self…
Holds all the answers I need
To keep me on the path I need to walk.

It only takes a moment
To ask…what is right for me..
To say the words of love I need to hear…
Sabotage is a word I will eliminate from my life..
I want what is best for me..
I care for others…
But I must come first in my life.

I am a beautiful child of the Creator
And deserve the best life has to offer.
Love is the answer…
Unconditional love…
Of my whole being!

November 2002

WHERE IS THE LIGHT?

For many a month a bright light shone within me
It would dim for a while…
And then would reappear even brighter…
It was as if the light shone from above
And illuminated me.

The light seemed to affect everyone around me…
Love flowed from me…
And returned in abundance.
My energy was continually replenished…
Ideas flowed…
The world was a wonderful place.

Over this past year…there have been numerous changes
In my life…so many positive forces at work
A new love…additions to my family..
A new home..
I could go on and on.

But there have been other changes as well..
Relinquishing some of my independence..
Letting go of an old love…
Shifting in family relationships..
Seeing loved ones slowly dying..
To name a few.

So many adjustments…so many changes
Changes mean adjustments and sometimes pain..
Acknowledging one's emotions is positive
But this can be draining and sap one's energy.

The last few weeks have been a struggle..
The light that was so strong

Has become dim.

There is fear arising within me..
The old way was more certain..
There was no relationship to worry about..
No one to answer to..
I could almost predict my daily existence.

Now. . . every day is different..
The path is ever winding..
Where is the light.?
Where is my inner peace?

I need to refocus
Look to my higher power for help..
Take more time for me..
To meditate. . . to read..
To just be me..
I have become lost in the process.

I am on bended knee
Asking Him. . . (I know he has not abandoned me)..
To enter my heart. . .
To be an integral part of my being.

Slowly, I feel the light return
I feel calm and peaceful
And oh so loved!!

February 1997

GUIDANCE

Yesterday I asked for assistance...
For guidance to help me on the way.
I wanted to speed up my healing
To proceed with my life...
To have less strife.

And last night
I had a dream...
Not the answer I wanted
But my dream told me so much.

As I went around in circles
Trying to solve the problems in my life
Often relying on my partner to guide me
To make my life easier...
Somewhere in the maze I was separated from my partner..
Left alone...to fight the battle.

Standing alone is frightening..
Sometimes I
feel I need someone beside me.
Holding my hand
But this may not be the answer or
What is best for me.

It can be frightening...
As in my dream...
Standing alone
Facing my fears
But I have the answers...
If I confront my fears..
Instead of running away
I'll be able to proceed.

It won't be easy..
But I'll succeed
For I have strength and courage
Good teachers
And strong intuition.

I may not receive answers
In the way I used to...
For my pattern is changing
I am learning to ask for what I want
And watching and listening for the answers I receive

Yes, life can be scary..
But never boring...
There is so much to experience...
So much to enjoy
Open your heart and your mind...
To the wonders in store.

January 2000

LOVE IS BEAUTIFUL

From the depths of my soul....
I cry...I pray...
I want things to change...
I need to change...

Things can't go on the way they are...
I surrender...leave it...
And move on...
and then once more I surrender...
And still my life is in turmoil.

When will there be peace?
Where is the serenity that was once part of my life?

I am bombarded with my reality...
Tossed to and fro...
It must be something I'm doing...
Or something I'm not doing???
What is the answer?

And a voice from deep inside..
Whispers ever so faintly...
You've been here before...
You have the answer...
You alone hold the key.

You can run from pillar to post..
Creating chaos...
The answer is not outside...
But lies within you...

Take the time to stop and listen ...
Listen to your heart ...

And you will know!!

And I ponder...
What could this mean!!

And suddenly there is a knowing...

Yes, I felt this way before...
When I lost a loved one...
I fought the impending loss..
My world was torn to shreds...
Darkness was all around...
And I struggled to survive.

Forcing myself to say goodbye...
When for me...this was not the answer.
Time healed the wound...
And gradually I let go...
But it wasn't a goodbye.. ..
For me...I needed to say..."see you later".

I know that my love never diminishes..
It is the essence of who I am.
It's form may change...
A loved one may move on..
Or possibly go to the other side...

But they will always be a part of me..
I have been fighting the essence of who I am...

My heart has a strong message...
And my head, the voice of reason, another...
Its time for them to align...
It's OK to feel...
It's OK to love...

Everything in God's time...
And I will heal...

And a peace surrounds me...
A calm like I have never known...

Love is beautiful...
Is there anything more????

July 2002

WHY

Someone asked me a question today..
A question that rocked me to my very core
"Why wasn't I doing something.....?"
For example...working further on publishing my writings...
Sharing my gift with more people.

This question has been nagging me ever since.
And as I take pen in hand
I know the answer...
Delving further into my writings is taking a risk...
Venturing into the unknown.

Where I am right now is relatively comfortable..
I have joy...I have pain...
There is happiness...some sadness..
I write...I share my works..
With a limited few.....
Probably those who accept and appreciate
And don't question!
I don't have to defend myself.

How many times in my life
Has it been like this????
I do what is relatively comfortable
Taking a risk...financially...emotionally...
Is so frightening.

And the greatest lesson I learned today is
Something I know from the bottom of my soul.
I'm worth so much more!!

I have a gift..I share it..
But the gift is meant for so many.

Becoming well known...
Which in my heart I know could happen...
When I dare to venture forth with my creativity....
Is so scary.

I'd rather be in a corner
Listening to others...
Reading their works
Studying their ideas...
When I know intuitively
That I have so many answers
I could write a library
That would help so many.

So when someone asks me "why"
..Why not share this gift?
...Why not venture forth?
...Why not go for it?
I have to look it square in the face
And act.

I am no longer as comfortable
As I once was...
Sitting on the sidelines
Listening to others.

I have a point of view
I have important lessons to teach...
Others to learn
And the teachers and pupils will appear..
I'm only delaying the process.

And I give thanks to a true friend
Who questioned "WHY?"

July 2000

ASK

There are times when I ask for something
And I know not why.

I feel an emptiness...
That something is missing in my life.

If only things could be different...
If someone could be in my life...
It would make me feel complete!

If my life were more exciting...
Then I would be happy.

And when I have had all of this
I often didn't realize what I did have...
The gift that I'd been given.

And today when I asked for Love in my life
For things to be different...
I received my answer.

I have to be complete within myself
To feel a great love for myself.
Love that comes from within me
And from my higher power

Then, and only then, will I appreciate
What is around me
The gifts that I do have.
The love that I have to share.

Situations change...people come and go
The only constant is me!!!

I need to focus on the wonder
And joy that is **ME.**

Christmas is a time of birth.
And, for some of us...
A miraculous time of rebirth
An opportunity for each and everyone of us
To be reborn in love.

I'll grasp this opportunity...the greatest gift
I'll ever have.
To begin anew...filled with love.

December 1999

THE CORE OF MY BEING

I run from pillar to post, at times so certain
At others doubting my decisions.
My focus is on the external...
My actions depending on what is around me.

When I am connected with the core of my being
I feel so warm, content and so loved.

To make a true response...
One that reflects my values and beliefs
I must focus on my inner being
And trust my gut reactions ...what is best for me.

As I focus on my inner being
I feel warm and tingly,
I ask a question...
"Why is everything around me so chaotic?"
And my inner being responds...
"You can only control your inner self..
Relax...meditate and you will cope.
You cannot change the outer world
Or the people in it."

Whenever I need an answer...
I ask the core of my being
"Is this right for me? ...How should I handle this?"

In my interactions with others,
Connecting with my core
I am more loving...
Yet taking care of myself.

My inner being is full of infinite wisdom...

I have all the answers.

From my inner core...
I respond with love and trust...
With appreciation of myself and others.

My responses are from the depths of my soul
And through my connection with the Creator.

As I connect with the core of by being...
I connect with all of humanity!!!

October 2007

RELATIONSHIPS

As I venture on life's path
I appreciate the connections... the relationships...
The circle of friendship and love...

The chance encounters...
Meeting my soul mate...

Becoming one with the universal family...

And walking with my Creator!

A MOMENT IN THE GARDEN!

Beauty is all around us...
In the sky...the clouds so blue..
The wonders of nature...
The changing season...
The people we meet...
The innocence of youth...
The wisdom of our elders.

Who can say what is more breathtaking...
Beauty is in the eye of the beholder!

Today I was given the opportunity to view a photo...
Which touched my heart.
The photographer captured a moment in time...
And caught the serenity of the scene..

Two ladies are sitting on a bench..
Their backs towards us...
Surrounded by a beautiful garden...
They look so comfortable.. So serene.

My eyes became a lense
And I zoomed in on these women..
I saw majesty, maturity, love,
Humour...a lifetime of caring and sharing...
They are obviously good friends...possibly sisters.

And I felt a longing to be a part of the picture...
But I stood behind...
Feeling the rapture...that only age brings..
The laughter...the jokes...
The silence...the familiarity..

The maturity to appreciate their surroundings...
And the ability to take the time..
To enjoy the moment.!

Beauty is everywhere..
But the moment in the garden...
Will be forever in my heart!

June 2002

FRIENDSHIP

Life would be so simple
If we could get beyond the colour...
Race or creed - to discover
What is being offered
By another.

Often people meet
On the street....
And feel no vibes
While others simply say hi
And they relate.

Some friendships are instantaneous
While others evolve...
Imagine the mutual joy
Of meeting someone who complements you...
Your ideas seem to mesh.

Does it seem ideal
Am I being a fool...
To feel that I have discovered
That rare someone
Who has the ability to uncover
The best in me!!!!

Some friendships are for life
Others are meant for times of strife.
But I'd rather have one friend
Who accepts me as I am
Than many acquaintances
Who know me for what they think I am!!!!

April 2001

MOTHERS

As Mothers' Day fast approaches
I sit here thinking of my Mother
And what she means to me...
The fond memories I have of her..
Memories that grow stronger every year.

I often wish
I had told her more often
How precious she was to me...
And thanked her for
Her love...
Her kindness...
For being my Mom...
For being there...
And having the courage to be herself.

She knew...I feel it in my heart...
How much I cared
But in our family...
We hesitated to say...I love you..I care.

This is a lesson for me..
For all of us
To take the time to say ....
I love you..You're special
To those we care about.

I think of my Daughter
So far away..
Wishing I could be with her
This weekend...on Mothers' Day.
And yet, I know
We are together

We are connected
As only Mothers and Daughters can be.

And I thank God for the privilege of being a Mother
We have our children for a short time...
They grow up and move on...
They are a gift to us...
Merely given to us on loan.

And I say a special thank you
For my Mom
I know we'll be together on Sunday
Happy Mothers' Day
I love You!!!!!

And to all the Mothers
Happy Mothers' Day
Thank you for the love you give
You enrich the world.

May 2000

TO DAD

You hold a special place in my heart...
An idea pops into my head...
Something I'd like to share...
I reflect for a few moments...
And see your smile of approval..
Other times it's a slight nod of the head...
Advising me not to proceed.

You were my mentor...as well as my parent
Your love was unconditional
And I never doubted how much you cared!!!

You were a person I often tried to imitate
But you taught me to be my own person..
To value my strength and integrity.

Possessions were never important to you..
Reading was your passion...
The quest for knowledge..
You were ahead of your time...
Your insight...your perspective on life...
Were timeless!!!

The love of your life was your family...
And that love has carried over to all of us..
We have many memories, Dad..
And your legacy lives on...

I know that you and Mom are looking out for us..
Laughing with us...
Crying with us...
Shaking your head...
Wondering when some of us will learn...

And then you sigh...
And say...
They will learn in their own time...
That's what life is all about...
Growing, learning and loving each other.

How I wish you were here...
To celebrate Fathers' Day ..
And yet you are with me every day of the year.

As I write this to you Dad...
I pen a wish to all Dads...
And Grandads..
Children and grandchildren...
On this special day....
Have a great day!!!

Enjoy each moment with your families...
Don't wait for Fathers' Day to celebrate...
To say I love you.
Make your memories
Each moment of your life!!!

June 2002

PARTNERSHIP

Partners are friends
Who wish to be together...
To grow together
While they share their lives...
Through love and caring...
Through the good times...and the bad....
Through the laughter and the tears!!

This friendship provides an open ear
And an open mind...
Learning to listen...really listen
To what is said...the tone...the words
One word can mean so much...
And actions...tell all!!!

This merger is an alliance between two...
A pact that allows for unconditional love....
There's forgiveness ..
Forgetting words spoken in haste or anger...
Letting go of old hurts
And starting anew...

Putting the past behind ..and
Living in the now....
It takes patience...persistence and
Most of all prayer...

Committing your relationship
On a higher level
Brings love and joy

Yes, there will also be pain and sadness
Adapting to one another...

Learning the other's needs
While retaining your identity....

Change is never easy....
Growing pains are necessary....
In order for the relationship to blossom.

It's not always a fifty-fifty venture....
The percentage doesn't matter
It's the results that count....

Partnership - a merger between
Two people who love each other...
Who strive to form an alliance
That lasts forever..........

February 2000

CHRISTMAS WITH THE FAMILY

Christmas with the family
I can hardly wait!

It seems only a year or two ago
We were together
Enjoying our Aunt's wonderful cooking
And basking in the love and camaraderie.

We had such good times..
It's great to reminisce.
And this year is part of the joy..
Of Christmas past,,
Of Christmas present..
And many Christmas celebrations
Yet to come.

And each year brings change...
One of my nieces and her family
Have moved into their new home...
I can visualize us sitting there...
Full of holiday goodies...

One or two of us chatting!!???!!...
And of course...
There will be laughter...
And love in abundance...

So if we hear an echo or two..
And wonder at the joy...

We'll close our eyes
And remember

Christmas past…

The clan gathered at the farm...
The musicians in town.

So many celebrations together…
Holiday conversations on the phone.
And through the years
Love has kept us together
Even when we were miles apart.

And now the cycle takes us to a new home…
And the wonder of the season
To celebrate…
To feel the love and warmth

Christmas with our family…
A time to remember
And keep in our hearts.

December 2005

FIFTY MORE

I sat before the fire
Gazing at the blazing flame...
My fingers gnarled
My eyes sometimes cloudy
Wrinkles on my face
But still not a hair out of place.

A proud old gentleman approached..
Hesitated and asked to sit down beside me.
He took my hand...moved closer
Slightly shaking and
Looked into my eyes.

He cleared his throat and uttered a sigh...
A small laugh of delight
Marney, he said
Do you know that you've been the love of my life?
You're more beautiful than the day we wed
Fifty years ago.

I lifted my head ...
Tears falling on my cheek
And the years instantly fell away from his face.
John - I replied..
You're that young boy
I fell in love with
So many years ago.

I've been in love with you always
Through our triumphs and despairs.
And you're still the love of my life.
And every day I thank the Lord for giving me you.

Would you grant me one wish...
Love me for fifty more!!!

January 2000

OUR DARLING GIRL

And the Creator blessed us
With a beautiful girl...
So precious...
So perfect...

And the tears flow as I think of her
What a miracle..
What a joy to behold.

She is a magnificent gift for all of us
To share..
Her beauty indescribable..
Her scent so precious..
Her aura like an angel.

And at this moment
Her big sister,
Momma and Papa
And the boys...
Are bonding as a family.

And I had a brief glimpse of this family
As I delivered dinner tonight...
And I felt a giant pull at my heart strings...
And the love flowed...
Along with the tears...

And I knew that I had been given
A gift
More precious than gold...
A wonderful family
To share...

For at least a little while.

And I thought of my Mom and Dad...
And their joy when our daughter was born
And I know that they are looking down...
And I can hear Dad saying...
"My Girls"...

Seeing them ...the wee family together
Brought back so many happy memories
And I know that I am truly blessed.

And I will have the opportunity to see her grow..
To watch my first grandchild...
The big sister now...
Show the new baby the way!!!

And Momma and Papa
Will do just fine..
I have no doubt...
For their love flows like a fountain
It's there for everyone!!!!

The precious one
Will teach us to truly feel
To connect..
To truly know the meaning of unconditional love.

For my girls...
My daughter and her children..
I give thanks for the wondrous gift
Of having you in my life...
And to you Papa
For being a significant part of our family.

And the circle continues...
The circle of love...

What joy…
What amazement..
To be a part…
To have the privilege of sharing!

Our precious one…
I love you…
You have touched my soul with your beauty
And I am truly…truly grateful
That I can share the precious gift
Of your presence.

You are a glorious child of the Creator!

October 2004

YOUR BEST FRIEND

When you feel lost and alone...
When the house is empty and
You have no where to turn...
Your pup comes running...
With tail a wagging...
Ready to give you a lick.
A fond welcome...
And the day is suddenly bright!!

On a cold winter's night...
You can cuddle with your pet...
Feel the warmth and caring
And you know that you're loved.

Such unconditional love...
Such caring...
You can do anything and
You're still loved.

On a rainy day...
When you'd like to stay curled in front of the fire...
You take your pup for a walk...
A bit reluctant, oh yes...
And yet you feel great...
Because you're together.

I could go on and on...
But words are not necessary...
From one pet lover to another...

September 2001

AUNT MARION – MY SOUL MATE

I kneel in silence
In solemn reflection
Of what you have meant in my life....

An aunt, a confidante and loving friend
Someone...some place where I could go
And there would be no conditions on love.
Yes, everyone should have an Aunt
For another name for Aunt is LOVE.
She loved life, and her family and friends to abundance...
She was love and she attracted love.

As all those who knew her would attest
She cared for one and all...
And her open door and bounteous meals
Reflected her love and caring.

They say we all have soul mates
And she and I were two...
We shared many a joke and
Laughed together for hours.
Uncle would shake his head....
But he knew the love we shared and
He was never excluded.

We laughed and cried together
And she was always there.

My Aunt has been in my life
From the day I was born
(just a year or two ago)
She and her brother (my uncle)
Helped keep my sister and I in line.

When she married our Uncle
And their children eventually joined the Clan...
Our Family was enlarged.

She kept opening her arms to include
Family and friends....grandchildren, nieces and nephews...
Were all part of her family.
The walls of her home and her heart expanded
To include us all.

Yesterday I stood beside her bed
Wanting to keep her in my life
Yet knowing...I had to let her go
I talked to her...like I've talked
So many times before
...What happened yesterday...
...What we were doing today..
And told a wee joke or two.

I talked of Grandpa, Grandma,
And of my Dad, her Brother
And that they were waiting for her
With open arms
And not to be afraid...
For He would take her by the hand.

Let go Aunt (I said)...
You'll feel no more pain
We love you so...how much you'll always know
And suddenly... she was gone...from this life.

The sun shone
And I knew that it was a message from her...
I'm here and it's a wonderful place.....
And the bright glow was her cheerful smile!!!

She's preparing a place for us all....
We know her so well!!

We bow in reverence
To one who has meant so much...
No one can ever replace you.
You are love and you are loved.

You'll always have a place in our hearts.

February 1997

JAMIE

I heard a voice from above
Calling...
Calling your name...

It was your Mother looking for you..
This beautiful magnificent presence
Spoke to me
Talking of her struggles...
Her illness...
Her love of her family...
And her journey "Home"

She has an eternal family now..
Family and friends surround her.

She is healthy...
Finally at peace
Happy yet misses
Her family - You and your Dad.

She wants you to know she sees your every move...
Feels your pain
And would like to carry it for you.

You are an extension of her...
Her beauty will continue to shine through you.
Be still and she will come to you...
In the quiet of the night...
Or on a walk through the park.

She is with you always...
Loves you unconditionally...
And will forever be your Mother.

She carried you in her womb
Was a constant strength while you were growing
And in recent years you helped carry her.
And now she says…
Jamie…rest on me awhile..
Know that you are loved…
And that this love will last throughout eternity.

Je t'aime…
I am with you always.

May 2007

DISCOVERIES

The Wisdom of the Ages

It's inside each of us.

Listen...
Take a moment in silence...

And you will hear the answers

A WOMAN'S WORTH

A woman's worth
Can never be measured...
On any scale.

As I learn to love myself
I experience a type of love
I have never known before...
I'm first in my life...
I start to pamper myself.

I listen to the child,
As well as the woman inside
Sometimes I agree..
Sometimes I argue..
Sometimes there is laughter,
Other times I shed a tear.

But no one can put a value
On me–I am unique
I am me......

But I am part of a larger force
That binds all of us together!

As I grow,
That love that is inside
Encompasses my whole being
And eventually affects those around me.

Yes, my worth is immeasurable
I believe in myself
I know I can survive
With direction from above

The anger, the fear are leaving me.

A woman's worth..
A person of love and inner beauty
IN THE HANDS OF GOD!!!!

September 1995

MY EMOTIONS

I remember a day when all was dark.
I saw others laugh and wondered why..
Others cried and it was foreign to me..
I looked in the mirror and saw a stranger.
Her face so drawn
Where was I?? Where had I gone?

I was in the depths of despair...
A depression..the doctor said.
And the days were dark..
And the nights much longer and darker.
It seemed there would never be light.

One day I listened to music..
The melody reached me
And touched my soul...
I felt my heart flicker...
And from that day there was hope.

A new dawn was approaching
I looked out the window and felt a tear on my cheek..
The tear, to me, was a diamond..
I had feelings buried deep inside...
And they started to surface...
And a wealth of diamonds
Ran down my face...
In a never ending pool.

From that day forth
The darkness began to lift...
A fraction at a time.

After the tears..
Began the fears...
The fear of going outside
Of trying new things...
Of living.

And yet I continued...
Each day a struggle...
For I knew the value of these feelings...
Coming from a place where there were none.

I released the feelings...embraced them...
And let them go...
Not for me was the answer
To be found in a pill..food or drink...
Each new feeling...each new emotion was the Creator's gift.

One day I laughed and the whole world
Laughed with me.
What a joyous feeling
To feel happiness.

The person in the mirror
Had shed 10 years...
And was beginning to look familiar..
It was Me!!

And the rest is history
From the depths of despair I recovered...
And today when I try to stuff my feelings...
I remember a time...
When I had none.
And give thanks.

The tears on this page...
Represent the wealth in my life...
The wealth of my experiences...

The replenishing of my heart...
The hope and courage to continue.

Each emotion is a gift...
A feeling...a message from my inner core...
I feel from the depths of my being...
I love with passion
Laugh with joy...
Embrace challenges...
And kneel on bended knee
Giving thanks for my emotions.

November 2002

AN ECHO FROM MY SOUL

As I listened to the recording...
I heard an echo from my soul....
Calling me...
Calling me....

"Listen...
Listen...
You are so beautiful...
So loveable...
No matter the wrinkles on your face...
The size of your waist...

You will always be a
Magnificent child of the Creator
You are unique.

Your beauty
Shines throughout the Universe."

And I cried
And cried....
And felt a warmth
And a sense of belonging...
Like I've never felt before.

No matter where I go
Or what I do...
These words will go with me...
The love...
The beauty...
The wonder of me...
Is breathtaking...

And I close my eyes
And sigh…
A feeling of contentment…
Surrounds my being.

And love is everywhere!!!!

March 2007

THE DIFFERENCE IS ME

I've come to a point in my life
When I'm looking at the picture..
The picture of my life to date
And wondering why.

Why am I here?
What have I accomplished?
Why have I made so many mistakes??
There have been failures of relationships...
Loss of friendships and so much more..
Why does this picture look so grim?

And then I focus in on me
And I see my beauty...
My potential waiting to be explored

I want to make a difference
To feel like I have a mission in my life.

For I'm not about loud noises..
Or applause...
Or great feats.
I can only be me...
That gentle voice
Beginning to speak out for what I believe
Reaching others through my writing.

I am making a difference
The mistakes...the failures are lessons for me...
Difficult lessons to face..
To learn from and go on.
Showing how vulnerable I am
And yet so loving...

Willing to try again.

From this day forth
Whenever I focus too long on my mistakes
Or am held in a vice by my fears...

I'll look at the picture that is me
The beauty...the love waiting to be explored
And say..Thank you God ...

For having the courage to be me
Looking at myself
And saying I'm okay
I do make a difference
Because I can be me.
And the difference is ME!!!

April 2000

INTUITION

Life is so exciting
When you allow your intuition to guide you.
Take the time ...a moment or two in silence
To stop and listen...
And a little voice will whisper the answer.

It may be an answer to a question...
An answer to a prayer...
The answers you receive
Are the guidance that is best for YOU!

As you learn to love yourself
Ask for what you want...
You know what is best for you.
Take the time in contemplation...
Asking for guidance..
And when you receive the answer
Proceed.

External distractions and advice from others
Is often deceiving
You have the answers...
Learn to trust yourself.

And somewhere along the way,
You'll feel so excited...
Exhilarated to discover...
That what you ask for
The things that are best for YOU
Will come your way.

And sometimes...as you evolve
You'll receive responses...

On topics that you've only dreamed about...
Or you have the thought...
And the answer is there.

A time spent in silence...
Praying for guidance
Is the answer to increasing your intuitive powers...
Trust...believe...
And the future is YOURS!

January 2000

A WEE VOICE

I heard a wee voice
Ever so softly whisper..
"Come out and play with me..
Won't you play with me?"

I often felt strange sensations...
A tap on my shoulder...
I'd turn around
But no one was there.

Or a tiny giggle..
The sound of a happy child...
Such a wonderful sound!

And today...I dared to really listen...
To pay attention to what was happening...

I closed my eyes...
And saw a beautiful child...
So happy...so full of life...
Running in the meadow...
Laughing...and beckoning me
To join her.

Would I dare!!
I look a leap of faith and followed her...
I ran and romped in the meadow with her...
And we laughed...
How we laughed!!

Felt the wind in our hair...
Tumbled in the grass...

And I felt so alive…
Truly alive…

We ventured by the brook…
I held her back…
She was so adventurous…
Wanting to jump in…

We took off our socks..
Dipped our toes in the cold water…
how we shivered…
And shrieked…
And yet we laughed
from the bottom of our souls…

What a delight…
What magic…
What an adventure…
To be with a small child…
And to become as a child…

What a wonderful feeling…
The love that flowed between us…
Was unconditional
And everlasting.

As I rested by the brook
Shutting my eyes for only a moment…
I heard her whisper..
"Bye….
See you soon".

I opened my eyes …
She was gone…
And I was sitting in my living room…
Alone…yet not lonely…
Feeling so content…and so loved..
I felt whole and complete.

Any time I want to
See my wee friend...
I have only to close my eyes...
Call her...
And she'll be there...

Ready to play...
To romp...
To be with me...
With her joyful giggle..
Her delightful smile...
And her love of life...

A lesson to be learned...
From a small child...
Run in the meadow..
Walk in the rain
Sing to your heart's delight..
Enjoy each moment
And simply be
A child again!!.

Listen for a wee voice..
Or feel a tickle...
She's there ...waiting!!

May 2006

AND A SOUL CRIES

And from the depths of my soul
I feel a connection to the Universe
To the women who are part of Creation.

I feel their pain. . .
Their joy
We are joined.

As I heal
They will heal!

Join Hands
And sing songs of love..
Of Peace
The songs will heal the world!

I love you unconditionally
Love you. . .truly love you
And my soul cries
Hear me
Believe me
And love me, too.

And a cry echoes from afar
I love you unconditionally
I love you. . .love you
Feel my love
Feel my caring
And know we are one.

And my soul was in awe
And a feeling of rapture
echoed through my body.

We are one
We are joined
We are love
And together we will heal the world

A soul cries
And the world answers
Love..eternal love.

And a feeling of warmth surrounds me
And I am enveloped in the arms of
the women of the world

January 2003

IN THE GAP

I decided to rest in the gap
To be in the here and now
To simply be
And I am going there now.

So I pause…and I am there…
In the gap…
Feeling calm…
And yet wondering…

How to fill this gap…
That will be in my life…
To fill the void..

And I feel a deep love
Reaching from my inner core
Telling me I'll be OK…
It's about finding where I really belong.

To feel confident in myself…
To love myself…
For my strengths, my wisdom
And what I have to give.

After the door has been closed…
There will be new opportunities in my life
New doors will open.

What door do I select?
Do I select Door 1 – The Poor Me Syndrome?
NO – I'll grieve the change –
but my life is not about "poor me".

Door #2 – As I open the door
I hear heavenly music
and a golden light surrounds me.
"Meditate my dear
Trust in yourself..
Listen to your heart
Trust in the divine and
You'll find a new path…
Part of love is to give…
Give of yourself and
You shall find your way".
Door #2 is a door I will open often
Leading me to heights in self-awareness –
in being and in doing.

Door #3 – I open the door
and melodies from my heart echo.
There are scrolls on the wall..
Scrolls from ancient times…
Scrolls from the scribes…
And at a desk an old man with a pipe
Beckons me to approach,

"My dear, you are needed here
Your words . 'The Echoes of Your Soul' –
must be preserved for all mankind…
For all eternity."

And with a tear in my eye I listen to him…
Knowing that he's giving me the courage to proceed…
The knowledge to follow the dream I've always had.

Door #3 – I can have access to the scribes at any time
And with this assistance my writing
will be preserved for centuries.

Door #4 – I hear the bagpipes play
and see green heather.

And I have traveled to a distant land.
This door encourages me to travel …
To visit new places…To venture forth…
To carry my truths…
And a way *will be found* so that I can venture forth!

Door #5 – Letting go!
Letting go of fears
Letting go of the past
Letting go of possessions
Letting go of the need of others' approval.

This is a new path on the journey called life…
Starting as a baby…experiencing life as a young child.
Laughing…running..playing…
Taking time to enjoy life
This is my time..to learn who I am
To be happy….to be truly me.
This is a powerful door!

Door #6 – Education – Growth
I see an ancient university…the sign of truth.
"You are always learning my dear.
We welcome you here…to grow…to learn…
But your gift to us is your talent…
your writing..
Teach a class…show what love is all about."

Door #7 – Faith – Hope – Charity
And the greatest of them is Love.
"Reach out my dear…
Project your love to one and all…
And ye shall receive in abundance"

And as I awake from my meditation…
From that place within the gap…
I feel renewed.
Knowing that I can go there any time..

And when I venture there…
I may open the door I desire.

In the gap…what a glorious place to be!

October 2003

THE SONG IN MY HEART

And I cried from the depths of my soul
Cried with such happiness
For finally I saw..
Finally I felt
My worthiness
What I am intended to be!

Only when I write
When I reach to the depths of my being
Do I ever really feel connected.

And this morning...at dawn
I read some of my writings
From a different time
And I was transported back...

And I felt such peace
And knowing...
That I am where I am meant to be
That I have this tremendous gift
That is meant to be shared

And I feel such joy
Such gratitude
And a knowing
That my words will be heard
That my books will be published
And that the universe will share in my joy!

And the Creator smiles
For I have finally realized
The essence of my creativity..
The wealth of my knowledge..

The depth of my potential...
And the tremendous gifts I have to share.

And I am finally singing
The song that is in my heart!!!

April 2004

DESTINATION

Life is for Living..
It's not how long you live..
It's what you put into life.

Not how far you travel
The dollars you accumulate.

It's how much you give to others
And most of all. . . how much you give yourself. . .
How much you love yourself..

The joy you allow yourself this moment is the answer!!!!

BECAUSE I AM ME

When I walk I stare at the earth
I never see the sky
I have never been able to walk tall
To say who I am
When will I hold my head up...and shout
I'm proud to be me.

I am a beautiful person
My face may not be that of a model
But it tells a story
Of who I am
I have walked many miles for someone else
Now I must walk for me.

I need to hold my head up
And look at the stars
To feel that I am free to explore....
What life has to offer.
I alone can make the difference in my life.

I'm me...I'm beginning to like myself
Some day I'm certain there'll be love.
I have so much to offer the world
My talents, my love of nature
My life experience
The special way I smile
I am unique...there will never be another
Just like me.

I am going to be free
I know that I've grown
Look at the shadow on the horizon
That's me!

I am looking towards the sky
But now I don't walk...I have learned to fly
Because I am me!!!!

October 1992

LIFE IS FOR LIVING

If today were my last day...
I'd jump in my car and drive as far as I could...
I'd look at the scenery...stop by a brook...
Maybe even take a drink or two.
And feel how fortunate I am..
To be able to see the beauty
To know that there are so many miles ahead.

I'd drive on..
At times listening to music..
Other times hearing the whisper of the wind.

It's been sunny for so many hours
And then, the clouds burst.
The rain starts...the wonder of the changing sky.
I'd better slow down...my foot tends to get heavy..
With so little time to drive...
And so much to see.

And as the rain intensifies, I realize that I must stop..
So reluctantly, I pull over to rest a while.
Why has the weather spoiled my journey?
I wanted to drive everywhere...to see everything...
And, just like every other day...
Something is preventing me from doing what I want!

I see an old school house ...it doesn't look threatening..
And what the heck, this is my last day...
So I might as well live dangerously!!

I bravely walk to the door and open it..
And it's as if I'm in another time and place.
I'm that little girl on her first day of school.

A brave smile on her face...
The girl with red pigtails and a freckled face
And a long dress to hide her shaky knees.

There are little desks...all in a row
I'd say twenty or so..
A wood stove stands in the corner at the back of the room
And a large chalkboard dominates the front of the room.

It must be recess because there is no one there..
Or perhaps there's no school today.
I decide to sit down...a tight fit..
(For I'm no longer a little girl).

And on the chalkboard in bold letters, I read.

"Life is for living
No matter how long you live..
It's what you put into life that counts.

Not how far you travel...
The dollars you accumulate...
Nor the sum of your accomplishments!

It's how much you give to others..
And most of all, how much you give yourself...
Love yourself...
The joy you allow yourself this moment is the answer!"

And as I sit in that little seat
Tears streaming down my face..
I realize my answer!
Yes, I have only today...maybe just this hour.
I can never see or do everything I want.

But the peace and love I feel at this moment
Can give me joy and happiness no matter where I am
Or where I go...

Whether it be around the world or across the street..

This peace and joy can fill my heart
If I choose to enjoy the moment!
To realize this my last day on earth, how ironic...
Yet how wonderful...
For I may never have known this miracle!

September 1998

AND I SOARED

And I soared through the air
My destination I knew not where…
I was on automatic pilot
And my soul would lead the way.

I traveled through time and space
Glimpsing various scenes from my life…
My birth…
My daughter's birth…
My granddaughter's birth..

And yes…I saw some of my friends
On that wondrous journey to the other side.
Their faces were filled with awe…
This wonderful place they were going…
They were heaven bound…
They were going home…
And I longed to join them.

But my journey took me back in time
To another lifetime…
I was traveling in an ancient land…
Fleeing for my life…
Several friends by my side.

And then I was in a native village…
Teaching school…
Teaching the children to read English.
But I seemed to be learning more from them…
A schoolmistress…so prim and proper…
Was learning what life was really about…

And then my journey took an abrupt turn

And the flight became rough…
Like the rough spots in my life…
And I was venturing into the future…
Into the unknown.

And a white light guided me forward…
Leading me into a strange land…
Somewhere I had never been before…
And I was in front of a lectern…
Speaking to a large audience…
To people from many countries…

And my message was…
The journey from my soul…

I had no fear…spoke of my experiences…
My love of life…my greatest teachers…
And I was surrounded by the volumes
Of my works….

And as I finished speaking…
The crowd rose in applause…
They heard my soul's songs…
For I had learned to speak my truths

And from there I journeyed to a mountain stream…
And reveled in the tranquility…
And felt totally at peace…

The journey into the future at times was calm…
Other times there were storms in the air…
But I stayed calm and
Accepted what came…
I left it up to Him.

And what a lesson to learn…
I am not in control…
My soul has the answers…

Because I am linked to our Creator…

If I go with it…
And accept the hands I am dealt…
The waters will become smoother
The transition easier…

And as I soar through life…
Knowing not where it will lead…
I feel a sense of adventure…
Simply to be!

October 2003

HOPING AND DREAMING

I can feel it
I can touch it!

I am on my way to
Where I belong
And I am grateful
Excited and emotional,
My feet barely touch the ground!!!

It's taken a lifetime
A lifetime of hoping and dreaming.
And only a moment
In time
Since I acted on these hopes and dreams.

And the reality...
When I actually see my book
In my print
Will bring me even higher

And to me this means,
"Anything is possible...
My dreams can come true."
I see them...
I feel them...
And am taking the actions to make them happen.

After this exercise
After seeing my first book in print..
I will have truly learned to fly..
Soaring to a newfound freedom!!

April 2007

JOURNEY THROUGH TIME

I looked into my eyes today
And I saw to my very soul.

It was a wondrous experience…
It seemed like I reached my soul in an instant
And yet part of me
Felt like I journeyed through time.

I saw the essence of who I am
And I was so humbled.
I saw the wisdom of the ages…
As related by an ancient scribe.
I saw beauty that only unconditional love
Can portray..
I saw love for all mankind…

I felt this awesome love for me…
It engulfed me…
Wrapped me in a cocoon of splendor
Far surpassing any experience of this world…

It lifted me higher than the clouds….
I traveled through space and time..
And suddenly angels raised their voices
In a heavenly chorus as the harps played.

The journey to my soul…
The journey of a lifetime…
Cost not a penny…
But made me a millionaire…

My soul told me stories I longed to hear
Of glories…

Of wonders…
Of my beauty…
And how much I am loved.

My soul said …
"You alone know your truth
Take the time to listen…
And you will acknowledge this truth…
Live it…and fill the world
With the wonders of your gift".

And as I sit here in contemplation
Of this deep spiritual experience…
I am still wrapped in the cocoon of love…
That surrounds me and
fills every pore of my body.

In an instant I traveled to my heart's centre…
To the soul within me…
And I found peace…happiness…and love.

October 2003

MY DREAM

I awoke and I was surrounded by blackness...
The blackness reached to my soul
Calling me to rise...
To follow...
The light flickering ahead.

I walked...I flew...
Venturing toward the light...
And felt no fear...
Only anticipation...
wondering what was happening...
Where I was going?

I felt a warmth within
That grew to a fire encompassing me...
I flew through time and space...

And entered a place I had only dreamed of...
I was surrounded by light...
That warmed me to the core..
And felt a love...I have only dreamed of..

And knew that I was Home
Where I would be forever safe and secure...
A place of peace and tranquillity

And the heavenly harps played..
The most wonderful music I'd ever heard
And my heart opened to the rapture...
To the joy of...

Being here...
Being surrounded by love and light...

Feeling so serene...

And the angels began to surround me...
Welcoming me...
And I knew that I'd been here before...
That I was not a stranger...
That I would never feel alone...
Or abandoned again...

I had reached my lifelong dream...
To be at peace in my home...
The place where my heart has always been...

And I revelled in the wonder
Of these feelings...
Floating on the endless clouds of love...

And then the darkness reappeared...
And I was back in bed...
Was it a dream...
Or had I really been...
HOME????

And often still, when I close my eyes
I see the light..
The angels surrounding me...
And I believe it wasn't a dream..
That I was Home...
If only for a little while...
And that one day I will be there again...
Never to return to my earthly home.

November 2002

SING YOUR SONG

Learn to live
Every day to the fullest...
To see the beauty in each moment...
So many of us never learn to sign our song!!

We have each been given the potential
Our own special gift to bring forth...
To enhance who we are...
To make an impact in our unique way..

Through the humdrum of everyday life
We often focus on our positions...
What we think we need to do...or be...
And never reach the essence of who we are...
And what we have to offer the world.

Take a moment to visualize..
To dream.. if you wish...
Listen to your heart...
What would I do with my life
If nothing was stopping me????

I see myself..pen in hand
Autographing my first book...
While on the Oprah Show
Is this reality...or only a dream!!!

Only I can make it come true...
I'm on my way...
I recently autographed
My first published writing.

I have started to hum...
That wondrous song that is in my heart!!

March 2001

YOU ARE THE KEY

You are the key..
The key to the Kingdom...
The key of creation..
You will lead the way.

Close your eyes and focus
Focus on each breath you breathe
The miracle that is yours
Feel the breath reaching
Every part of your being
The breath of life..
Divine life.

Picture each breath...
The Creator's rays...
warming your body
Golden rays of love.

Focus on the love
Entering every part of your being

You are indeed one of the miracles of the Universe
Each ray of love entering your consciousness
Will shape the world.

Use this love wisely
You have the key to open the door
Only you know the answer..
Which door will be opened.

What is the divine wish
that you will experience..
This wish will be yours

Believe in the power of your being..
Believe you are made in God's image
Your power is infinite.

Each moment you live
Each breath you breathe
Each thought
Each decision
Will change the world.

For you are the key
To eternal happiness..
Love and peace.

You are indeed holy.

The power within you
Will revolutionize the Universe.
Thy will be done.

Open you eyes
And begin creating
For the power is yours
The destiny is yours

If you believe
That you are the Key!

April 2004

MY PURPOSE

And when I question
Why?
What is my purpose?

I only have to reach within
And find my greatest joy...
My greatest fulfillment.

For when I write...it's like turning on a tap...
And words flow from my soul
And my soul writings are created.

And as the flow continues
I feel my body's reaction
Tears flow...
My heart opens
And my soul cries.

Yes, my soul cries...
Because it is happy and content
To be heard
To sing its song
To echo the words for all eternity.

Soul writings...
Echoing from within...
Are my connection with the divine...
With the universal energy..
My reason for being.

The words flow...and a writing occurs
For me...and for all
Who wish to read...
For from these writings

Comes a universal song...
A message of love and hope
A feeling of gratitude and humility
And a divine sense of being.

For many a year I have questioned
Why?
What is my purpose?
And closed an ear to the answer.

I have asked to be published..
To be famous...
To be on the Oprah Show..
When what matters to me...
Truly matters is...
to make a difference
If only to one person..

And through the depths of my being
I acknowledge that I am making a difference
To myself and to those who read
The echoes from eternity...

The words of love
Will never be silenced
And I feel a peace within my heart
For I am where I am meant to be
Writing...truly appreciating
The gift that I have been given..
The miracle that is in my keeping..
The joy that I can bring.

Soul writings by the Universal Scribe - Marney Jamieson
A depth of knowing..
The beauty of creation
And an act of divine love!!!

June 2004

www.ingramcontent.com/pod-product-compliance
Ingram Content Group UK Ltd.
Pitfield, Milton Keynes, MK11 3LW, UK
UKHW020142200726
13856UKWH00003B/810